THE STANDARDBRED HORSE

by Charlotte Wilcox

Reading Consultants
Standardbred Retirement Foundation

CAPSTONE PRESS
MANKATO, MINNESOTA

C A P S T O N E   P R E S S
818 North Willow Street • Mankato, Minnesota 56001

Printed in the United States of America.

Library of Congress Cataloging-in-Publication Data
Wilcox, Charlotte.
    The standardbred horse/by Charlotte Wilcox
    p. cm.--(Learning about horses)
    Includes bibliographical references (p. 45) and index.
    Summary: Examines the history, characteristics, and uses of the
    American Standardbred horse.
    ISBN 1-56065-467-8
    1. Standardbred horse--Juvenile literature. 2. Standardbred horse--United
States--Juvenile literature. [1. Standardbred horse. 2. Horses.] I. Title. II.
Series.
SF293.S72W45   1997
636.1'75--dc21

                        96-46930
                          CIP
                          AC

Photo credits
Standardbred Retirement Foundation/Courtesy of Monica
Thors©, cover, 10, 30, 33; Courtesy of Ronni Neinstadt©, 8, 20
Dan Polin, 6, 42
Faith Uridel, 12, 18, 22, 36, 38-39
Cheryl Blair, 14, 26
International Stock/Chad Ehlers, 17
Lynn Stone, 24, 29
Unicorn/MacDonald, 34
FPG, 41

Table of Contents

Quick Facts about the
Standardbred Horse

Description

Height: Standardbreds stand 14 to 17
                 hands from the ground to the top
                 of the shoulders. That is the same
                 as 56 to 68 inches (142 to 173
                 centimeters).

Weight: A full-grown Standardbred weighs
                 about 900 to 1,200 pounds (405
                 to 540 kilograms).

Physical
features: Standardbreds are fast trotting
                 horses. They are tall and have
                 long legs.

Colors: Most Standardbreds are dark
                 colored. They are brown, black,
                 chestnut (reddish brown), or bay
                 (reddish brown with black legs,
                 mane, and tail). A few are gray or
                 roan (white hairs mixed with
                 dark).

Development

History of breed: Most Standardbreds descended from a great harness horse named Hambletonian 10 (Ham-buhl-TONE-ee-uhn TEN). His father was a Thoroughbred. His mother came from a line of trotting horses.

Place of origin: Standardbreds came from the eastern United States.

Numbers: About 750,000 Standardbreds are registered with the United States Trotting Association. More than 12,000 are added every year.

Life History

Life span: A well-cared-for Standardbred horse may live 25 to 30 years.

Uses

Standardbreds are the fastest harness-racing horses in the world. They also pull buggies for Amish people who do not believe in driving cars. Some Standardbreds become riding horses after they retire from racing.

Chapter 1

The Harness Horse

The Standardbred horse is the best harness horse in the world. A harness horse is any horse that pulls something. Standardbreds usually pull buggies. Because the breed was developed in the United States, Standardbreds are also called American Standardbreds.

The Standardbred breed was established on its ability to travel quickly. A horse could be a Standardbred only if it could meet a speed standard.

Standardbreds can trot very fast. They have strong legs and hard hooves. More Standardbreds pull buggies and racing carts than any other horse breed in North America.

The Standardbred is the best harness horse in the world. They are sturdy horses that can trot very fast.

The driver controls the horses with long, leather straps called lines.

Driving a Horse and Buggy

Driving a horse with a buggy is different from riding a horse. A buggy horse does not wear a saddle. It wears a harness. Straps from the harness attach to the buggy so the horse can pull it. The driver sits in the buggy. The driver controls the horse with long, leather straps called lines. The lines attach to a bit. A bit is a piece of metal that is put in the horse's mouth to signal it to stop, start, and turn.

Driving a horse is harder than riding one. It takes years of experience to become a safe driver. The horse needs careful training to become a safe harness horse.

Types of Harness Horses

Any horse that pulls something is a harness horse. There are large harness horses and medium-sized harness horses. The large ones are called draft horses. They are very strong. They can pull heavy loads. But they are not very fast.

Medium-sized horses are better for pulling buggies. They are faster than draft horses. A horse that pulls a buggy is called a driving horse. Many different breeds make good driving horses. The fastest is the American Standardbred. They are the fastest harness horses in the world.

Chapter 2

The Beginnings of the Standardbred

The Standardbred history started more than 200 years ago in England. Lord Grosvenor (GROHV-ner) owned a great Thoroughbred named Mambrino (Mahm-BREE-noh). This horse descended from another great horse called the Darley Arabian.

Mambrino was a fast trotter. He could trot faster than some horses gallop. He was a great harness horse. Lord Grosvenor once bet that Mambrino could trot 14 miles (22 kilometers) in an hour. No one accepted the bet.

Niatross is one of the most successful and popular Standardbreds of all time.

Messenger

In 1780, Mambrino was bred with a Thoroughbred mare. A mare is a female horse. She gave birth to a gray colt. His owner named him Messenger.

Messenger was not a harness horse. He was a racehorse. Messenger retired from racing when he was eight years old. His owner sold him to a man from the United States.

In 1788, Messenger arrived in North America. He lived the rest of his life in Pennsylvania, New York, and New Jersey. He was a breeding stallion for 20 years.

Messenger was a riding horse. But he was bred to harness-racing mares. Their sons and daughters were fast trotters like Messenger's father, Mambrino. Messenger's offspring became harness-racing champions.

Messenger died in 1808. He was 28 years old. He was buried at Long Island, New York.

Messenger's offspring became harness-racing champions.

Chapter 3

The Development of the Standardbred

One of Messenger's sons was Abdallah (Ahb-DAH-lah). He was bred to the Charles Kent mare. This mare did not have a name of her own. In those days, some people called horses by their owners' names.

The Charles Kent mare was a trotting horse. She was from Orange County, New York.

Their foal was born in 1849. The owner named the foal Hambletonian 10. At that time, harness racing was very popular. Most harness-racing horses were Morgan horses. Morgans are a breed of horses from one famous stallion from Vermont. Hambletonian changed the idea

Standardbreds came from crossing Thoroughbreds with other breeds that could trot well.

that harness-racing horses were always Morgans.

Hambletonian's offspring were faster than Morgans. Morgan owners started crossing their horses with horses that had Hambletonian blood. Soon, anyone who wanted to win a harness race had to have a Hambletonian horse. Hambletonian had 1,335 foals. They were born between 1851 and 1875.

Most Standardbreds living today trace their ancestors back to four of Hambletonian's sons. They were George Wilkes, Dictator, Happy Medium, and Electioneer. George Wilkes was born in 1856. Dictator and Happy Medium were born in 1863. Electioneer was born in 1868.

During those years, breeders were developing two types of harness horses. These two types still race in harness today. They are trotters and pacers. They do not race against each other. Trotters race against other trotters. Pacers race against other pacers.

Trotters and pacers do not race against each other. They race only the same kind of horse.

Trotters and Pacers

All horses have four natural gaits. These are the walk, trot, canter, and gallop. The walk is the slowest. The trot is next fastest. The trot is a medium-fast step. Horses can go for long distances when trotting.

The canter is faster than the trot. It is a slow run. The gallop is the fastest gait of all. But horses become tired when they canter or gallop. Then they must slow down for a while. At a trot, a good horse can go many miles or kilometers without getting tired.

When trotting, the horse moves its feet in a certain way. One front foot moves at the same time as the back foot on the opposite side. The trot is an easy gait for horses. They make good time without using too much energy.

Some horses can learn another gait called the pace. They get the ability to pace from their parents. Only some Standardbred horses can pace. Those that can pace pass this ability on to their foals.

A gait is the way a horse moves its feet to travel.

Harness horses are trained to pace or trot, but never gallop, when they pull a cart.

The pace is different from the trot. The front foot and back foot on the same side move at the same time. The pace is a little faster than the trot.

Trotting and pacing are the best gaits for pulling carts and buggies. But when most horses trot or pace very fast, they want to break into a gallop. Harness horses must be trained to only trot or pace, but never gallop, when they pull a cart or buggy.

Setting the Standard

Some horses trot or pace naturally without breaking into a gallop. In horse-and-buggy days, everyone was looking for this kind of horse. Hambletonian horses were the best. They set a new standard for fast trotting and pacing.

Around 1870, some breeders started a registry of trotting and pacing horses. They wanted to keep track of harness-horse pedigrees. A pedigree is a horse's family tree. The registry was called the American Trotting Registry.

The new registry set a time standard for trotting or pacing a mile. If a horse could trot a mile in two minutes, 30 seconds, it could be included in the registry. For pacers, the time standard was two minutes, 25 seconds.

A horse that could not meet the time standard could not be registered. Everyone wanted to use the faster, registered horses for breeding. They called them Standardbreds.

Chapter 4

The Record Setters

Standardbreds became the top harness horses in the world. They won more races than any other breed. Soon, they were the only breed on the harness racetracks of North America.

But not all Standardbreds were racehorses. Hambletonian's son Dexter broke a record in the 1860s. He trotted a mile in two minutes, 17 seconds. Robert Bonner bought Dexter for $25,000. Bonner refused to race him for moral reasons. They drove him just for fun.

Standardbreds were bred to be faster and faster. In 1897, Star Pointer paced a mile in one minute, 59 seconds at Readville, Massachusetts. It was the first time a horse had traveled a mile in less than two minutes.

Standardbreds became the top harness horses in the world. Soon they were the only breed on the racetracks.

The Great Dan Patch

The most famous Standardbred was Dan Patch. He was born April 28, 1896, at Oxford, Indiana. He was a bay stallion. Dan Patch paced his first race on August 30, 1900. He won every race that day except one. A New York man bought him for $20,000.

Dan Patch became world famous. He set more records than any harness horse in history. Once, he broke two world records on the same day.

In 1903, Marion Savage was looking for a good racehorse. A friend of his saw Dan Patch at Kansas City, Missouri. The friend could not wait to tell Savage about him.

Savage paid $60,000 to buy Dan Patch. He went to live at Savage's farm in Minnesota. He lived in a huge, fancy barn. Savage hired a famous horse trainer to handle Dan Patch. The trainer was Harry Hersey.

Savage and Hersey loved Dan Patch. They made sure he was never overworked or abused. He never entered another race again. Instead, he paced in exhibitions. People paid money to see Dan Patch pace.

Dan Patch was a great bay stallion like this horse.

Standardbreds win more races than any other breed in the world.

Exhibitions

In an exhibition, a pacing horse races around the track with a running horse. The running horse gallops. It does not pull a cart. This means the running horse can go faster. The exhibition horse tries to keep up with the running horse. This keeps the show exciting, but it is not truly a race.

Dan Patch set a world pacing record of one minute, 55 seconds for a mile. This was at Lexington, Kentucky, in 1905. He paced again on the same track in 1908. This time he almost broke his own record. But the running horse had problems.

Dan was pacing behind a running horse named Cobweb. They went three-quarters of a mile in one minute, 25 seconds. That was faster than any horse had ever paced. They had a quarter mile to go. All of a sudden, Cobweb started to slow down.

Cobweb was hurt. Dan Patch slowed down to stay behind him. Hersey was driving the cart. He had to turn Dan toward the outside of the track to get around Cobweb. Dan kept going, but he lost time. He did not break his record.

World Famous

Dan Patch became world famous. Many people loved him. Restaurants and taverns were named after him. There were Dan Patch brand-name products. Songs were written about him. There was even the Dan Patch dance step.

Huge crowds came to watch Dan Patch pace. He received $21,000 for one exhibition. He traveled the country in his own private train car. He earned more than $3 million during his life.

Dan Patch traveled until he was 15 years old. Then he lived five quiet years with his owner in Minnesota. Dan Patch died on July 14, 1916. Marion Savage was heartbroken. He died the next day.

Trotting Associations

In 1871, the American Trotting Register started keeping pedigrees of all Standardbreds born in North America. The Canadian Standardbred Horse Society started in 1909. They keep a separate Canadian registry.

In 1939, the American Trotting Registry joined with harness-racing clubs. They changed their name to the United States Trotting Association. The Canadian Trotting Association began the same year. These groups

Two trotting associations were started to keep track of the family trees of all Standardbreds in North America.

make rules for harness racing. They give out licenses for trainers and drivers.

Chapter 5

The Standardbred in Action

It has been more than 100 years since the first standard time was set. Modern horses trot and pace much faster. Today's Standardbreds can do a mile a whole minute faster than the standard of a century ago.

In 1993, Cambest paced a mile in 1 minute, 46 seconds. He was five years old. In 1994, Pine Chip trotted a mile in 1 minute, 51 seconds.

What Standardbreds Look Like

At first glance, Standardbreds look a lot like Thoroughbreds. They are tall and have long

The trotting associations try to make sure Standardbreds are not mistreated.

legs. But most Standardbreds have bigger bones than Thoroughbreds. Many have longer bodies.

Most Standardbreds are dark in color. They are brown, black, chestnut, or bay. A few are gray or roan. They have long manes and tails. Their eyes are large.

Standardbreds are medium-sized horses. They weigh about 900 to 1,200 pounds (405 to 540 kilograms).

A horse's height is measured from the ground to the withers. The withers are the spot at the top of a horse's shoulders. Standardbreds stand 14 to 17 hands. One hand equals four inches (10 centimeters).

A Standardbred's hindquarters are very powerful. This gives the Standardbred its speed when it trots or paces. They have strong muscles in their upper legs.

Another reason Standardbreds can run fast is their breathing. They open their nostrils very wide. This brings plenty of air into their lungs. They need a lot of air when they are racing.

Most Standardbreds are dark in color.

The Harness Race

Harness races take place on an oval racetrack. The oval is usually one mile around. People watch the races from bleachers around the track. Horses pull two-wheeled carts called sulkies (SUHL-keez). Drivers wear brightly colored outfits called racing silks.

The horses do not line up in starting gates like Thoroughbreds. The horses and sulkies ride onto the track. A truck drives slowly in front of them while they trot or pace. The truck has a long gate attached behind it. All the horses line up behind the gate. Then the truck quickly pulls away. The horses take off, and the race is on.

There are separate races for trotters and pacers. Each race is called a heat. Eight or more horses and drivers race in a heat. Horses can race several heats in one day.

Standardbreds start racing when they are two or three years old. A good Standardbred may race for 10 years or more. This is a long

Harness-horse drivers wear brightly colored outfits called racing silks.

Standardbreds make good family horses when they retire from the racetrack.

time to race compared with other breeds. A Thoroughbred might only race for three years.

Standardbreds can race longer because they do not race at the gallop. Galloping at racing speed wears a horse out. Standardbreds also tend to have stronger bones and feet than

Thoroughbreds. Standardbreds who start racing at an older age do not become worn out as quickly.

Life After Racing

Buying, training, and caring for a racehorse is expensive. Most owners keep only horses that win. If a horse is too old or too slow, the owner sometimes sells it. This can be a problem for Standardbreds.

Many people only think of Standardbreds as racehorses. They think Standardbreds do not make good riding or family horses. Not many people want to buy Standardbreds when they retire from racing.

Many Standardbreds are killed for meat when they can no longer race. Some become buggy horses for the Amish. The lucky ones are adopted by loving families.

Amish Life

Most Amish people are farmers. Many of them live in Pennsylvania. Others live throughout the midwestern United States and Canada. The Amish people live the way people did in the

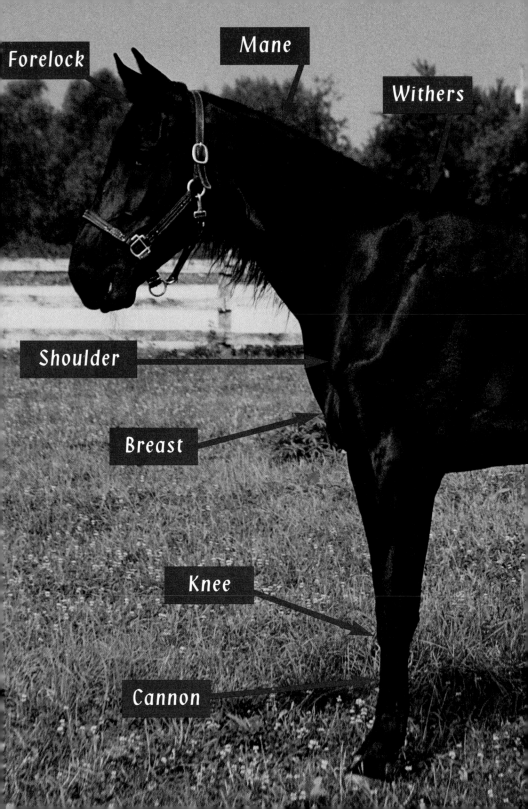

Loins

Hindquarters

Flank

Hock

Fetlock

1800s. The Amish do not believe in using modern machines or electricity. They do not drive cars or tractors. They use horses for travel and farm work.

The Standardbred is the favorite buggy horse of the Amish people. Standardbreds trot when they pull buggies. They can pull a buggy at about 10 miles (16 kilometers) per hour.

A Standardbred is known to be a sturdy horse. A Standardbred in top condition can trot farther that probably any other breed. That is why years ago they were often used for transportation.

In the 1800s, everyone drove horses and buggies. There were plenty of people to buy Standardbreds after they were done racing. But when cars were invented, only Amish people bought Standardbreds. Most of the rest of the horses went to slaughter.

Today, there are not as many Amish people as before. They need fewer horses. So more Standardbreds are sold for meat. But some people are trying to change that.

Many Amish people buy Standardbreds to pull their buggies and to help with farm work.

Rescuing Standardbreds

Standardbred rescue groups find homes for retired racehorses. Some publish newsletters and Internet pages. People can adopt a Standardbred. They save many horses from slaughter this way.

Standardbreds make good family horses. They quickly learn to pull buggies. They do well in roadster classes at horse shows. In these classes, the horses pull carts. The drivers wear racing silks. They trot or pace around the show ring at different speeds.

Now many people are using Standardbreds for riding. They do well on country trails and in fancy show rings. They compete in everything from rodeos to jumping classes.

Healthy Standardbreds are good at endurance riding. These events cover 25 to 100 miles (40 to 160 kilometers). They last several days. Standardbreds often win these races. Their strong, steady trot keeps them going. More people are riding and driving Standardbreds than ever before.

Standardbreds are beautiful horses that are good at a variety of jobs.

Words to Know

bit (BIHT)—a piece of metal inserted in a horse's mouth used to direct and control it

exhibition (ek-suh-BISH-uhn)—a show in which a horse exhibits its speed, but usually not against other horses

foal (FOHL)—a young horse

gait (GATE)—a way a horse moves its feet to travel

gallop (GAL-uhp)—the fastest movement of a horse

harness (HAR-niss)—the set of leather or nylon straps that a horse wears to pull something

harness horse (HAR-niss HORSS)—a horse that pulls a cart, wagon, or buggy

mare (MAIR)—a female horse

pace (PAYSS)—a special gait natural to only certain breeds of horses

roadster (ROHD-stur)—a small cart or buggy, or the horse that pulls it

stallion (STAL-yuhn)—a male horse

sulky (SUHL-kee)—a small, two-wheeled cart used for harness racing

trot (TRAHT)—a medium-fast step natural to all horses, easily recognized by its up-and-down action

To Learn More

Brown, Fern G. *Horses and Foals*. New York: Franklin Watts, 1986.

Edwards, Elwyn Hartley. *Encyclopedia of the Horse*. New York: Dorling Kindersley, 1994.

Henry, Marguerite. *Born to Trot*. Chicago: Rand McNally, 1950.

Henry, Marguerite. *One Man's Horse*. Chicago: Rand McNally, 1970.

Patent, Dorothy Hinshaw. *Horses of America*. New York: Holiday House, 1981.

You can read articles about Standardbred horses in the following magazines: *Hoof Beats*, *Horse Illustrated*, *HorsePlay*, *Practical Horseman*, *Young Equestrian*, and *Young Rider*.

Useful Addresses

Canadian Standardbred Horse Society
and **Canadian Trotting Association**
2150 Meadowvale Boulevard
Mississauga, ON L5N 6R6
Canada

Harness Horse Youth Foundation
14950 Greyhound Court, Suite 210
Carmel, IN 46032-1091

Standardbred Pleasure Horse Organization
31930 Lambson Forest Road
Galena, MD 21635
E-mail address: Janis.Comstock-
Jones@ecrknox.com

Standardbred Retirement Foundation
P.O. Box 57
Blairstown, NJ 07825
E-mail address: ttzd18a@prodigy.com
http://www.HarnessHorse.com/srf.html

Trotting Horse Museum and Hall of Fame
240 Main Street
P.O. Box 590
Goshen, NY 10924-0590

United States Trotting Association
750 Michigan Avenue
Columbus, OH 43215-1191

Internet Sites

Canadian Standardbred Horse Society
http://home.ican.net/~troton

HarnessHorse
http://www.HarnessHorse.com

Standardbred Pleasure Horse Organization
http://www.ecrKnox.com/gallifry/spho.htm

United States Trotting Association
http://www.ustrotting.com

Index

48